Project Earth

Volume 1

Susanne Edelmann

Impressum

Bibliografische Information der Deutschen
Nationalbibliothek: Die Deutsche
Nationalbibliothek verzeichnet diese Publikation
in der Deutschen Nationalbibliografie;
detaillierte bibliografische Daten sind im
Internet über dnb.dnb.de abrufbar.

©2024 Susanne Edelmann
Verlag: BoD • Books on Demand GmbH,
In de Tarpen 42, 22848 Norderstedt
Druck: Libri Plureos GmbH,
Friedensallee 273, 22763 Hamburg
ISBN: 978-3-7597-8787-3

Content

1. Preface

Please only read this book, if you know that it is aimed at you. If you don't know, consciously examine yourself until you know. This book is deliberately written for a specific group of people and if you are not one of them, there is no point in reading it. Rather, it steals valuable time from you that you can use for other things. However, if you know that you are a human part of the "Project Earth", we warmly welcome you.

If you are a human part of the Project Earth, your current life is a very complex life. A human life that was aimed at a single goal from the very beginning: your personal commitment to the Project Earth. However, you didn't know this and so, you blamed yourself when you didn't fit in so often and things turned out differently than you wanted. You doubted yourself when your love fell apart, and your friends moved away from you without you being able to hold them. You were often alone and yet, you fought with everything you had to belong and be a "normal person" like the others.

Yet, you increasingly distanced yourself from what is generally human; it often didn't affect you and sometimes even disgusted you. No matter what you tried, you could only change the described situation relatively.

Time and time again things seemed to slip away from you and things often turned out differently than you wanted. You took responsibility for everything and anything and as the years went by you became increasingly tired. The huge mass of social negativity has weighed on you. Your apparent inability to fit in, be a normal person, and live the life you wanted has allowed inferiority and self-doubt to grow. In addition, a lack of fulfilling perspective in your front has strengthened the increasing resignation that already existed.

The fact of complete unconsciousness has caused you enormous holistic damage. Purely objectively, viewed from the outside. And if the words we have just written touch you, we strongly encourage you to put the book aside for a while and consciously allow all related injuries to dissolve in the long term.

You are not a normal person. In fact, you never were. You are a highly developed personality in human incarnation, and it is high time you are fully aware of it. What's more, you are not just a highly developed personality, you are here, in this one human life, to support a very specific project.
For this task you have had to solve a wide range of, sometimes extremely complex, tasks over the last few years, without you even being aware of it.

No wonder, from a purely human perspective, your human life became even more unstable, even less suitable and overall, definitely "not very successful" in these last years. Your goals were far beyond human comprehension, and it seems now, time for you to be fully aware of this. You are a human part of the Project Earth and that is why you are here in this one human life. Your task in this regard is an incredibly high one and so, it deserves respect and appreciation. Please be fully aware of this now.

What we would also like to emphasize at this point: You are entitled to a human life that corresponds to your high mission. Please not only be fully aware of this, but also consciously allow it. You cannot organize said human life yourself, you probably know this by now. Yet, you can allow it very consciously. And that's what we ask of you.

If you look at the biography of your current life with a significantly broader perspective, you will be able to see that your essential task was to guide your lifeline. You had to do a lot of preparatory work in this regard and so, your life was led in such a way that you could carry it out as quickly and as successfully as possible. The rest was for your personal well-being, but very often also for various higher-level tasks that you also carried out on the side.

Your human self honestly had little influence on what was happening, even if you yourself had that impression. And if you like, allow a comprehensive look at this. So that you basically know and find some peace with your current human life.

Once you have integrated the relevant knowledge, it is advisable to maintain the open view described, as this will help you to classify things correctly. This makes your human professional career what it is: Completely irrelevant and yet, always helpful in order to be well anchored in human society, to have a completely normal human life on the outside and at the same time, to have a diverse and repeated impact on important human issues and to support other highly developed people on their path.

Once you have recognized this in depth, this will provide you with lasting relief and it allows your human self to let go better as it recognizes something much bigger.
Your essential task is not written anywhere, and it is not assigned to you or confirmed by any official body. You know it energy-based instead. Vaguely at first. And over time the power becomes stronger and stronger. If you now, consciously give space to this inner knowledge, you will experience how your essential tasks gains power.

Suddenly it is clear: Your (main-)job is your essential tasks. Therefore, by profession you are now an "active member of the Project Earth" and in your function you are at most an "active human SEOS member", "active member of the Light Technology Project in the Field of Human Health", etc.
Meanwhile, it may well be that you also have a human job and may also work independently at the same time. Typically, energy-based: Everything together. If you now, immerse yourself in the situation described using your expanded energy-based perception, you will easily see that the main energy lies in your essential task. The rest, which is what it is, happens incidentally and depends on your personal well-being and your essential task. Something that you cannot and do not have to consciously shape but is now continually developing. However, it will help you if you are fully aware of what is being described, as this will change your evaluation and perception. Something that is good for you holistically.

The focus is now on your essential task. Regardless of what else you do. And if you enter the energy of the Project Earth using your expanded energy-based perception, you will realize that a lot has happened in the last few months.

The energy-based realms have become significantly more involved and as a result the project has gained strength.
This relieves the human members and currently gives them the opportunity to establish a safe and beneficial foundation in the human habitat. And this too, is not the responsibility of your human self but lies entirely within the guidance of your own inner essential self. You can get involved with confidence, knowing that you will be guided safely and correctly over the next few months. Towards a holistically rich human life.

If you incarnate into a human life, you need many valuable years until you have matured humanly and mastered materially based humanly. Something you have to do again in every single life. And even if you move forward more quickly over time, you still waste valuable years, every time. Added to this is the fact that you then, have to overcome the path to complete awareness and master the two energy-based dimensions in order to actually be able to tackle the planned essential tasks. This again requires a lot of holistic resources and, in particular, a lot of time.

And since the first people now have a completely light-based human body, have successfully mastered the corresponding conversion and are able to lead a completely normal human life with their new body, we have decided to open up this possibility to as many currently capable people as possible. The corresponding conversion requires a lot of holistic strength and diverse skills. At the same time, it enables the respective people to have a significantly longer span of their current human incarnation and we would like to consciously use this in the current phase of the Project Earth.

Your holistic maturity, your diverse abilities and your stable, high vibrational frequency are of great service. And we are grateful for that!

Please be aware that the project is completely energy-based, is subject to energy-based circumstances and laws and that all communication is also energy-based.

"We" are in this book:
Susanne Edelmann / Lady Nayla Og-Min, Lord Luca / St. Germain, Lady Serena, Lord Ben Josef

May the book serve you and enrich you in many ways!

Sincerely
Susanne Edelmann / Lady Nayla Og-Min, Lord Luca / St. Germain, Lady Serena, Lord Ben Josef

2. Introduction

The Project Earth serves to sustainably and fundamentally increase the frequency of the entire planet, with the aim of significantly improving living conditions, especially in the third dimension, and thereby significantly reducing the negativity currently present there. The project very consciously uses energy-based evolution and changes in this regard at the highest possible level. All members of the project have the personal development level of a master, and most are sometimes very far above it. The client of the project is the Council of Light, the management and coordination of the project is the responsibility of the Galactic Federation of Light and they in turn, have set up a specific intergalactic project management group for this purpose. A group that has existed stably for several hundred years now and has acquired a lot of relevant specialist knowledge and experience during this time.

The management team is very well connected across the universe and was able to draw on a wide range of knowledge, skills and support. Seen in this way, Project Earth is a universal project in which countless personalities have contributed and continue to do so.

Since SEOS was consciously founded, the project has grown significantly in strength, as more and more of the earth's inhabitants are now consciously contributing and this can be unmistakably perceived in terms of energy. We assume that you carry your task in this regard purely and clearly within you. If this is not the case yet, put the book aside and let your own inner essential self show you them. Please also check whether you are one of those people who have (or will have) a light-based human body. The more conscious you are and the more you know, the easier it is for you to overcome the associated challenges. Not all human members of the project will have a light-based human body. It is particularly those who are active SEOS members or who work in the field of light technology who rely on it. But the conversion in this regard is extremely challenging and not all of the people who come into consideration are holistically capable of carrying out such a major conversion. And so, it seems important to us that you know. You, for yourself.

At this point we would also like to point out that energy-based projects behave significantly differently than human projects. And if you want to delve deeper into it, you will find what you are looking for in the book "Light Technology".

It seems important to us that you are aware that your effort is under the complete guidance of your own inner essential self. Your human self and your human mind have no influence whatsoever and so, it is honestly a waste of time if you are busy with your task in your human mind. He can't help you in this area. Your essential task lies beyond his comprehension and beyond his sphere of influence. If you want to know, we recommend that you consciously go into your essential task using your expanded energy-based perception and allow everything that is important for you to show itself to you.

You probably know by now that you always know sufficiently early. It doesn't need anything more from an energy-based perspective. It's continually evolving, and you know continually. As a rule, you only know your own part and you only concentrate on your own part. This allows you to be focused and effective, as it would be unnecessary to worry about things that don't concern you from an energy-based perspective. Energy-based projects behave significantly differently than human projects do, and we would like to address some aspects here.

2.1 Energy-based projects

Energy-based always opens up to you what serves you here and now. Preoccupying the mind with things that do not really serve is a human peculiarity that is not lived or understood outside of the human environment. Energy-based also opens up to you in principle according to your essential level of development. Naturally. Therefore, it can very well happen to you that, although you carry it pure and clear within you, that you are a human member of the Project Earth and also know about the big picture, the rest remains hidden from you. You don't need it, it doesn't serve you and so, you don't know. Logical, on an energy-based level. Unusual in the human environment and therefore usually takes some getting used to for a person.

In practical terms, the situation described means that you know your own part, that you roughly know the big picture in accordance with your own personal development, but that the rest remains hidden from you. You don't need it. Even within the framework of an energy-based project, you live the humility of the master, who knows his full greatness and at the same time, is also aware that he is always just a part of the whole.

Many a person currently calls themselves masters, feels and behaves big and powerful and teaches all sorts of things. However, you can recognize the true master by his inconspicuous appearance and his humility. One of the reasons why master beings are generally not recognized by people.

**Anyone who has to show outside
who he is,
don't really know yet
who he is.**

Finding one's own place in human society is a fundamental human-material-based task. This task involves various aspects that need to be understood and mastered. Once you have mastered the basic task and, over time, the entire material-based dimension, it is important to very consciously deal with the new and the respective differences.

When you are in the energy-based dimension, you have a comprehensive and fundamental understanding of who you are. Something that very few current people know. At the same time, this fundamental understanding also changes your behavior when living together and working with other personalities.

- You no longer have to prove yourself and you no longer have to work for or even fight for the place you deserve.
- You cannot "settle yourself" into simple tasks and you cannot get to a position at a high level in the hierarchy that does not really correspond to your current level of personal development and skills.

You need very high skills if you are elected to a leadership team of an energy-based project. Additionally, you need a very, very high integrity. You have to prove both of these numerous times in advance before you even come close to a possible selection process. Human behavior or even human ambition is therefore out of place in the area of energy-based projects. Rather, it forms instead. Naturally. According to the essential size and essential abilities of the respective personalities.

In the area of energy-based projects, your use is usually similar:

You know – you do – and you step back quietly.

Your use is therefore always controlled by your own inner essential self and is based on your own inner secure knowledge. You act accordingly. And then, you devote yourself again to your own life and other things.

If you are an active part of the Project Earth, this means that your current life continues as normal, and you continue to be an important and normal human part of human society. You influence the human environment, and you do this very often, well rooted in human society among the people. The human idea that your whole life revolves around the beginning of your essential task is therefore wrong. On the one hand. On the other hand, things are changing very clearly for you personally, as you can see that your essential task is taking on more weight and the rest of your life is being subordinated and adjusted to a certain extent.

If you are mindful, you will notice that you are the only person who notices this. For everyone else, everything seems to be going on as normal. And that's a good thing and will stay that way. At the same time, you will repeatedly experience relief from human tasks, you will have additional time for personal regeneration, and you will clearly understand the high importance of your essential task. All of this happens differently than is generally normal or cognitively thought, and so, you probably first have to experience it practically in order to actually know.

Energy-based is rewarded and it flows back accordingly. And this also behaves differently than usual in the human environment, and it will help you if you consciously let yourself be introduced and shown it to yourself.

Awareness contains great power and so, we encourage you to consciously allow yourself to open up wherever you still lack it. Energy-based tasks are currently not always financially compensated and that is why we think it is important that you know about the appropriate compensation in these situations. Essential tasks are not volunteer tasks, nor are you doing them selflessly "for good." Human attitudes that often echo again as soon as your essential tasks take up more and more space in your everyday human life.

With energy-based projects you receive not necessarily money as compensation. Nevertheless, you receive holistic compensation that suits your current needs

And if you like, let your own inner essential self introduce you to the topic very consciously. So that you know comprehensively and can be calm and safe in the new.

As a human being, you know "either – or". The energy-based dimension lives a fundamental "both and".
And like this:

- You do your work in a human profession and earn your money there.
- You are an active part of an energy-based project and receive appropriate holistic compensation.

And at the same time both aspects mix and there is the other in both.

You don't do a task as part of an energy-based project on the side. Instead, your everyday life is naturally organized according to your respective tasks. You also have sufficient resources available at all times. This happens naturally as long as you consciously let go and continually engage with your authentic inner impulses.

If you are connected to the energy-based dimension, planning and organization are no longer necessary. You now always have what you need here and now.

We have written repeatedly in several other books: Your basic mode of life changes significantly as soon as you are subordinate to the energy-based dimension. This fact also applies to energy-based projects, and it will help you if you fully understand the new situation that has arisen as a result.

Energy-based flows naturally into one another, as long as you allow this freely.

This is continually arranged according to your respective priorities and your respective authentic needs.

Your life mode changes fundamentally once you are subordinate to the energy-based dimension. Your external human life, on the other hand, remains more or less as it was before, even if it is a little more suitable in some areas.

2.2 Project Earth

If you planned to be an active member of the Project Earth before your current human incarnation, as you become more conscious you begin to have an inkling that you are part of a large energy-based project. At the beginning this impression may be a bit unclear and fluctuating. Over time, however, it becomes more and more solidified and at some point, you know pure, sure and clear: You are an active member of the Project Earth. A basic requirement for reading this book profitably, otherwise it makes no sense whatsoever.

If your essential tasks then begin to take up more and more space in your current life, it is advisable to ask very consciously about your current role (including the associated tasks) in Project Earth. Until you know this purely, safely and clearly within yourself.

There is no planning based on energy. It is continually evolving. Therefore, things are constantly moving, and you are always where you can optimally contribute yourself and your skills and at the same time continuously develop yourself. What happens to you is what serves you optimally. From a purely objective point of view, it is therefore pointless to impose any ideas on yourself or to compare yourself with others.

We have already written it several times: You no longer lead an average, normal human life. Therefore, a classification in this regard or a comparison with other, average people blocks you without promoting you in any way. However, it doesn't make sense to feel like you're some kind of superhero because you are part of a very nice and helpful project. You are valuable, that's true. You've done an incredible job. That's true too. Honor and appreciation automatically flow to you, and you can notice this clearly if you consciously pay attention to it. At the same time, the energy-based level is in many ways "emotionless" because it is not emotionally charged. And so, your essential size in the energy-based dimension behaves differently than is common among people and it is now important to become more and more aware of this.

In the energy-based dimension there is no evaluation and comparison. Instead, it is capturing and recognizing. Value-free and at the same time pure, clear and transparent. If you are subordinate to the energy-based level, your life and your basic attitude will also change in this respect. Something that repeatedly irritates those around you because they can no longer really understand you and as a result some attempts at classification are bounced off you ineffectively and empty.

At the same time, you become a strong projection surface. Your fellow human beings see their own issues in you and are no longer able to deal with them there, on and with you. This gives you repeated challenge. Challenge to look at yourself and work on yourself. Ideally, you are also very aware of this, as the various unpleasant behaviors of those around you do not change just because you are now subordinate to the energy-based level.

Your current life is your personal path and your participation in Project Earth is your personal task. You carry out your respective tasks under the secure guidance of your own inner essential self and you always know sufficiently early and sufficiently much. As a result, you don't need a lot of things on an energy-based level that you definitely need in a human environment.

However, you live both: Working in the area of a large global project and lead a human life and work in human tasks. Even if you engage in a variety of energy-based tasks, you are still human and your materially based human life takes up generous space until your last breath. It is important to be aware of this.

People have a tendency to "spiritualize" and thus to split off to a certain extent. Therefore, most of them have to learn, in the course of their personal path to consciousness, to root themselves well in matter and in the material based human living space. Yet, at the same time, they must understand that the energy-based dimension is a very real one.

When the energy-based dimension opens up to you, you increasingly begin to live in two dimensions at the same time, and this happens significantly differently than a human mind can imagine. So, you have to experience it by practically grasping. You yourself. Until you fully understand.

Project Earth consists of various segments, and we would like to go into these in more detail in this book series. This book will primarily deal with the basic aspects of an energy-based project and the aspect of frequency increase. The book lays the foundation for the next books, so to speak.
The core topic of the project is planetary frequency increase. A topic that has many facets and will accompany us again and again throughout the entire book series.

3. Planetary frequency increase

Together we are raising the fundamental frequency of planet Earth. Aware that all frequencies present here will automatically increase. Every increase in frequency has a lasting effect and so, the topic needs to be studied in detail and comprehensively before it is applied in practice. Every person who is actively involved in the area of planetary frequency increase is therefore, asked to study consciously and actively. Until he fully understands. We do not want to cause chaos or unrest with the project, nor do we want to cause any damage in any way, and so, we work extremely carefully and very consciously.

In order for you to become operational yourself, you need, on the one hand, comprehensive knowledge of the topic of increasing frequency, but on the other hand, you also need a very high level of awareness and mindfulness in your work. We don't need heroes or lone fighters. Instead, we need very conscious and capable people who know their own essential greatness and their own essential abilities and at the same time, are aware that they are always just a part of the bigger picture.

You must have harmonized greatness, power and humility within yourself, thus. Something that you know pure and clear within yourself as soon as this is the case. You also need to know your essential skills very well. In every way.

If you live in the energy-based and material-based dimensions at the same time and are subject to the energy-based dimension, you first only know energy-based. You know, although nothing of this is showing up in the material-based dimension yet. If you consciously enter your expanded energy-based perception in this situation, you can perceive the knowledge as an energy field in your environment. If you then consciously go into the energy field in question, you will receive further information that is important to you. Consciously give this information space within yourself and allow it to develop into your highest and best. As a rule, in the next few days, nothing will happen or change on your outside and your current life will continue to run normally and unchanged. However, if you go into the energy field of the new every now and then, you can notice how it becomes stronger step by step and is continually filled with new information. At some point, the first relevant piece of the puzzle will appear to be practically materially based and from this point on you just have to allow yourself to be guided internally step by step.

Energy based is very personal. And that's what you need to be aware of. You cannot transfer your own experience 1:1 to other people and you should no longer do so very consciously, at the latest once you have a personal connection to the energy-based dimension. Energy-based always happens according to the respective personal development status and the respective personal tasks. An energy-based teacher is aware of this and therefore teaches significantly differently than an average human teacher does. And if you have taught repeatedly in your life so far, it may be that you have repeatedly acted on an energy-based basis in this area and as a result have experienced some projections and some unpleasant things. If the words resonate with you, consciously allow this area to become permanently clarified so that you can be permanently free.

An energy-based teacher is consistently in the here and now, grasps in complex dimensions and always acts for the highest and best of the person in question. This happens outside of predetermined curricula or goals that other people have defined.

And if you are one of those people who have the ability of energy-based teaching, it will help you if you are aware that you are teaching outside of currently common human ideas. In this area too, all you need is your own complete awareness so that the outside of you becomes calm and secure. If it is clear to you, your fellow human beings can no longer burden you with their own ideas. Energy-based evolution also works in this area. For your own relief. And if you like, consciously take the topic with you into your next few days, observe consciously and allow yourself to be consciously introduced by your own inner essential self.

Frequencies can be increased in various ways:
- Your own high vibration frequency causes the frequencies of your surroundings to involuntarily move upwards.
- If you consciously dissolve stressful forms of energy or energy fields, the vibration frequency of the respective place, the respective topic, the respective system or even the respective person increases.
- Consciously work with high-frequency forms of energy or even with light also increases the respective frequencies.
- The conscious processing of stressful life events, but also the conscious dissolution of restrictive behavior or thought patterns also increases the frequency of the respective person.

- Life-enhancing frequencies such as laughter, unconditional love, liveliness, natural orders and healthy structures, etc. have an increasing effect on the basic vibrational frequency of people.

Any form of frequency increase involuntarily destabilizes and so, you don't go through your everyday life constantly increasing frequencies. On the contrary, sometimes you consciously lower these slightly in order to temporarily stabilize people or entire systems.
Increasing frequency is one of the essential tasks and is therefore entirely subject to a person's essential self.
Your human mind has no influence whatsoever and so, in the area of this task, you have to let go a little bit internally and consciously get involved in the guidance of your own inner essential self.

Increasing frequency loosens energy fields and forms of energy in human systems. And if you work in the area of frequency increase, your surroundings are often restless, unpleasant, difficult and stressful. The light-based human body supports you sustainably here: The unsightly things roll off you. Something you probably need to consciously experience a few times to fully understand. At the same time, this fact naturally repeatedly contributes to the irritation of those around you.

You no longer let yourself get caught up in emotions and those around you repeatedly feel like they are not being taken seriously or understood by acting out their own issues that they project onto you or other people. It visibly rolls off you and this is irritating. If you consciously continue to remain calm and clear, these irritations can no longer affect you. You are now well and comprehensively protected. Something we have been trying to achieve for several centuries and now, thanks to the light-based human body, we are finally achieving. Something that significantly relieves stress. Finally!

If you have a light-based human body, you naturally carry a very high fundamental vibration frequency within you. This, in turn, significantly promotes the planetary frequency increase. Wherever you are, you are increasing the vibration frequency there. Naturally. Just by being you. At the same time, your light-based human body multiplies your strength and power to work with light. And this fact also supports the planetary frequency increase. We ask you to consciously observe, to consciously allow yourself to fully recognize, so that you know how incredibly valuable and great you work. Please allow knowing fully. In all its details.

It is important that you fully know and understand yourself and consciously give space to this knowledge within yourself. If it is revealed in you, it will have a positive effect on your entire human life. Different than what you imagine with your human mind. Very different. And at the same time incredibly beneficial and valuable. For yourself. Only for yourself. Beyond human norms and ideas.

3.1 Project groups planetary frequency increase

We are now in the comfortable position that some people have reached their essential vibrational frequency in a stable manner and the number is increasing almost daily. Therefore, it is now, time for us to consciously start working in (additional) project groups. The first of these (additional) project groups started some time ago and we have already achieved some success in this regard. If you are part of such a project group, you certainly know this within yourself. You then, also know where you are specifically working, and you recognize your personal commitments.

We mostly work with light or vibrational constructs. Together, but also always individually. As a rule, the individual project members do not know each other and in most cases, they never get to know each other personally. Sometimes, when you work with others, you can capture their energy signatures and sometimes, you capture them as a personality. However, this is not really important. The commonality happens even without conscious knowledge.

With the exception of the personality who leads the project, of course. The entire project is based on their energy signature and frequency.

Internal communication is exclusively energy-based and so, you always know what you need to know. You are always in the right place at the right time and then, you know what your personal task is. It doesn't need anything more from an energy-based perspective.

At the same time, we would like to point out to you at this point that things are constantly moving in the energy-based dimension and are therefore, always different and happening differently. Materially based, over time, you can let yourself fall into a certain familiar routine and this gives you security. However, energy-based security lies exclusively within yourself and outside is always different. It is important to understand this fact, so that you feel comfortable in energy-based projects.

Energy-based projects are guided using frequencies and vibration and so, they are ultimately based on vibration. And you don't just have to be aware of this, you also have to understand the topic comprehensively. We work primarily with frequencies and vibrations and so, it helps you if the area becomes increasingly familiar to your human self and your human self also increasingly understands it. In his own unique way.

However, we not only work with vibration and light, we also, work through conscious transformation work. A work that can also sustainably increase the planetary vibration frequency. This work also happens individually and together. If you work together, you meet in groups and transform certain social issues there. The oppression of women, for example. But also, the topic of evaluation or control. You meet on a human, material basis as part of a human team or a human (travel, music, etc.) group and yet, at the same time, you are also an energy-based project group. As part of this task, in addition to the respective human tasks or priorities, you consciously address certain social issues and thereby, transform them sustainably.
In parallel, you usually implement new and beneficial solutions in the area of the respective topic. All of this currently happens far too often unconsciously and thereby, generates a lot of personal and group dynamic unrest.

Something that doesn't have to be the case, as all project group members have a sufficiently high level of awareness to be able to recognize comprehensively and therefore deal more consciously and calmly with the sometimes unusual or unpleasant situations and the side effects that arise repeatedly.

And if you like, consciously ask whether you are already in such project groups and, if so, let them consciously show you what you do there. The more consciously you know and live, the calmer your human self becomes and therefore, your human everyday life.

At this point, we would like to point out an energy-based fact that also takes place within the framework of the project groups just described: It opens up individually. Always the one that best serves the person. What you know clearly and purely is probably something that most other project members don't necessarily know. They don't need to know this either. Yet, you yourself know what you personally need, and which serves you optimally, and there are a lot of other things that you don't necessarily know because it doesn't serve you and you don't need it.

People often discuss and sometimes take the opinion that every team member needs all the same and thus all the information. The energy-based level also works differently in this area. There is no need for discussion or exchange of information. In the energy-based dimension you naturally receive the situations and information you need. You, personally. You, for yourself and for your tasks. The energy-based level focuses you. You, your well-being, your behavior, your tasks and your further development. Nobody outside has to take care of it. And therefore, the actions of your fellow human beings are not your concern.

If you are an active member of Project Earth, the reasons change why things happen.

And it helps you, if you are not only aware of it, but also increasingly understand and know it fundamentally and comprehensively.
- You repeatedly experience situations that contain themes that you transform through your conscious experience. These topics are not related to yourself, although it often seems that way.
- You are in certain places to support and empower certain people or strengthen them in their current frequency increase.

- You repeatedly find yourself in settings that require your high and pure frequency in order to be able to make lasting, positive changes.

If you are subordinate to the energy-based dimension, you are removed from the current world economic system. A matter that is currently still very unsettling, although at the same time, it is incredibly liberating. Meanwhile, you immerse yourself very consciously in the various relevant topics and transform and develop new, healing and free paths. You do this alone and together with others. You do this in association so that you succeed. And this logically tempts you to put yourself in relation to the respective situations.
Something you should very consciously avoid. Therefore, it helps you if you consciously repeatedly withdraw, enter into a conscious inner dialogue and allow yourself to recognize comprehensively. This is the only way you can do your essential work without harming your human self. It is important to be aware of this.

**You transform through
active living out.**

The topics you experience usually have nothing to do with you personally, even if it feels like it happens repeatedly (the cleansing / healing of femininity, for example). And so, you can always consciously get out of them, consciously cleanse yourself and take enough breaks.
Your awareness of this helps you not to get mentally caught up in the respective topics and not to let those around you relate you to the topics. People relate very often. A behavior that becomes void as soon as a person is subordinate to the energy-based level. The people around you are not aware of this. You, on the other hand, should be.

If you have reached your own basic vibration frequency in a stable manner and perhaps even have a light-based human body, you will usually perceive vibrations very clearly. You enter a building and would like to leave it as quickly as possible, for example. Although it looks beautiful from a purely material perspective, the forms of energy hidden there disgust you and the low vibration frequencies repel you.
If you now resist your natural urge and instead stand very consciously, consciously give space to your own essential vibration frequency and allow things to happen for the highest and best of all involved, your inner aversion will dissolve. You can stay and change in a stable way.
Yet, that's how we change.

The key lies in your consciously held own essential vibrational frequency and therefore, in your decision to consciously focus on yourself and your own frequency. If you instead, allow yourself to be distracted by your respective outside and concentrate on your appearance, you will lose your natural strength. And so, on the one hand, you need awareness in this regard. On the other hand, probably some conscious practical training until you fully understand and are able to consciously carry out the described task repeatedly without damaging your human self.

The biggest negative side effect of your use so far has been the various damage to your current human self. We have accepted this very consciously over the last few centuries. It was still unpleasant and stressful. Now we can consciously work through it one last time and then be permanently free of this challenging side effect.
The situation described has accompanied you throughout your current life and so, it may well be that you don't quite trust the new thing yet and expect it to be difficult and stressful again in your everyday human life. Totally understandable. Your experiences have clearly shaped you.

At the same time, however, you can now let them all go very consciously, observe them very consciously and carefully and recognize with ever greater certainty that things have visibly changed and will stay that way.

The core task of Project Earth is to increase planetary frequency. If frequencies begin to increase sustainably, there is an involuntary, lasting positive change. And we want to achieve this very consciously. This is typically energy-based: Circular, optimally adapted to the respective environment and without having to or being able to know the concrete results right from the start. The result is a lasting positive change and therefore sustainably positive living conditions for all living beings on the planet. At the moment, no one knows exactly what that will look like, in practical terms. And so, we would like to point out to you at this point that people are used to setting mental goals and very consciously orienting themselves towards desired, clearly defined results. A typical human behavior that does not serve you in the energy-based dimension and that you must consciously let go of in the area of energy-based projects. You can't say what exactly triggers your actions. And you have to (be able to) live with that.

At the same time, however, you can say with complete certainty that the effect is positive, and the change is for the highest and best of all those involved.

If you are mindful, you will be able to recognize that, from a human material perspective, the aspect described is a certain basic attitude and therefore, from an energy-based perspective, a certain vibration frequency. Said frequency is the basis of successful energy-based work.

Mental images block energy-based arising. They limit and very often make it impossible to achieve the best possible result. Not only do you have to be aware of this, you probably also have to "relearn" very consciously. You are blocking yourself when you "think and look forward on a human, material basis." A human behavior that mostly occurs unconsciously and at the same time, from an energy-based perspective, "diverts" energies. You consciously influence it and so, the energies cannot develop freely. The human mind is materially based and therefore, significantly limited when viewed from an energy-based perspective. And so, you use mental images to minimize the result that could arise, if it were energy-based and allowed to arise freely.

Energy-based develops on the basis of frequencies. Health is a high vibrational frequency and is based on high and pure frequencies, for example. Poverty is a low vibrational frequency and is based on holistic narrowness and a deep, negative vibrational frequency often tainted with dark forms of energy, as another example. If people were conscious, they could independently change their lives using frequencies. Most current people cannot yet do this independently.

You, on the other hand, do. Therefore, we invite you to do this very consciously in your own life. On the one hand as an energy-based role model, on the other hand as the basis for your personal abundance and your personal practical learning experiences. You can only teach what you know thoroughly. And this always includes self-experienced practice.

The vibration-based level is based on vibration and frequencies, ultimately. And any work, be it work with high-frequency energies, conscious energy shifts using vibration or even work with light, changes the respective frequency and therefore works according to energy-based evolution. At the same time, however, it is also subject to energy-based laws.

This means: If you work energy-based, you have no conscious influence on the respective effects. Basically, what develops is what serves the respective people or regions as much as possible. Always. At the same time, no one can consciously influence the respective result. Whatever serves the best needs happens. Naturally. People focus on (often mental based) results, performance and success. However, if you then, start to work energy-based, you have to consciously change your perspective and focus on vibration and frequencies: the initial frequency and the "effective frequency". The rest is beyond your control and beyond your responsibility. Yet, it is important to be aware of this.

3.2 Conscious change in social issues

In a human, material-based environment, you have to go into politics, (college / university) education or high management positions in order to have an impact on social issues. Of course, you may be involved in these committees. At the same time, we are making changes primarily based on energy, also in this area.

- We go into the respective topics in association, act them out and in this way, resolve them more and more.
- We transform negative forms of energy and restrictive human realities imposed in the respective topics or social areas.
- We keep our own high vibration frequency stable and thereby initiate sustainable frequency increases in the respective topics, which in turn makes lasting, positive and life-promoting changes.
- We consciously live out new, beneficial aspects and implement them for the first time in human society.

We're very grass rooted, so. We are and work where there is little light and there is little awareness. Our work is usually inconspicuous, as it is not obvious to most people what exactly we do.

However, you should be very aware of this at all times. On the outside, you are a completely normal person with completely normal human tasks. At the same time, you are a valuable and active member of Project Earth and whatever you do in your human life is based on this essential task.

Even if you are practicing a seemingly normal human job in the setting in which you are currently working, you will easily see that you are also working on Project Earth and are making lasting social change in the topic of your current place of work. You are there because you are explicitly needed in this place and in the associated topics. And since you are still a completely normal person, it will help you if you are aware of this topic.
This will help you to better classify and understand why you encounter certain situations that you have had little response to before. Said situations have no connection to you personally. However, it is about your essential task.
And especially when you consciously live it out, it is important that you know that the topics cannot be related to yourself, your personality or your character traits. Even if this connection is usually created in the human living space and you can catch some overlap in this regard in your important and valuable task.

Be aware of possible overlaps and resolve them very consciously. Also be very aware of your respective work and do it very consciously. Act out, knowing that this will lead to a lasting solution. Over and over again. Please do it very consciously without yourself relate the situation to yourself.

The task described is currently carried out by many people in an unconscious manner and as a result they repeatedly fall victim to accusations and incorrectly imposed labels and sometimes find themselves caught up in self-accusation, their own guilt or feelings of failure. A side effect that can only be overcome with increasing awareness. You must know who you are and why you are here and now in this one human embodiment. You need to holistically understand why you are in the places you are currently. And, you have to understand what you are doing, how you are doing it, and why exactly you are doing it.

It also helps you, if you consciously and continuously dissolve on an energy-based level what wants to get stuck in your personal energy space. So, that you are free and can continue working freely.

When a person reads "conscious implementation of light technology in the area of human health," they involuntarily associate tasks in the health area with the topic of "healing." However, human health is a holistic story and so, we are implementing it much more comprehensively and, in particular, much earlier than humanly thought.

People usually only react when their body clearly announces itself and already shows more or less severe symptoms of the disease. However, up to this point there is a long period of time in which a lot of bad and damaging things have happened. Things that could have been avoided if the person concerned had practiced conscious and mindful self-care. Therefore, health, energy-based and viewed holistically, begins with a very conscious examination of oneself.
This, in turn, requires energy-based teachers who are able to support people and accompany them in the long term into an essential and holistically healthy life with the highest possible level of self-empowerment. Thus, if you support in the area of holistic health, in the human living space, you are more of a teacher than a healer.

If you have the personal development level of a master in your core being, if you have reached your essential vibration frequency in a stable manner and if your holistic being is connected to the energy-based dimension, your practical life will be "multi-track".

You have "several tracks" in your head.
On one you perceive the energy fields and overlays and thus the thoughts of other people. On another you perceive your own thoughts. Yet, on another level you "hear" any energy-based communications from energy-based personalities.
Once you reach a certain level of awareness, this happens to you without any prior warning, and you would do well, to be aware of it and also to learn very consciously to tell the three variants apart and to be able to assign them to the respective "soundtrack".
People have a lot of thoughts about you. And the higher your fundamental vibration frequency, the more strongly you can perceive them. If you recognize them for what they are, you can find your own way of dealing with them. Ideally, you dissolve them in an energy-based way, so that they can no longer be thought about you.

You recognize your own thoughts because they are authentically connected to your current feelings and needs. Other people's thoughts are somehow connected to you and your current life, but they have no connection to your inner self. This distinction helps you to consciously recognize in the first phase.

Over time, however, you will be able to notice the difference based on energy. Other people's thoughts feel much less dense than your own thoughts. In terms of energy, they have a significantly weaker filling.

Even if you can consciously distinguish between them over time, we still recommend that you consciously dissolve any extraneous thoughts that you can perceive. Otherwise, they shape you unnecessarily and thereby repeatedly weaken you.

Energy-based communication also has its own filling, viewed from an energy-based perspective. And if you are mindful and aware, you will recognize them clearly over time. People have the unpleasant habit of speaking into the lives of those around them without being asked. And people who have recently died usually retain this habit for a longer period of time. The respective messages can be helpful. However, they can just as easily be empty and worthless to you. Only you can recognize the value.

Things are different when a master personality speaks into your life. He also usually speaks without being asked and very directly. Words that have a very direct connection to your here and now and touch on topics that you should revisit. Maybe you have to consciously experience this form a few times until you recognize it for sure.

If you meet another personality in the energy-based dimension and communicate with them in an energy-based way, this usually happens in the form of so-called holograms, and thus, you suddenly have a "whole book of information" in your head. And once you have consciously experienced this form a few times, you will definitely recognize it at any time. Of course, your counterpart will too.

You live several lives at the same time.
If you are fully conscious and subject to the energy-based dimension, you can create your completely perfect human life. Yet, you do this, to a certain extent. At the same time, your current life is following the path of your essential task, and you know this within yourself.

Said essential task is so big and sometimes unreal that you keep "rejecting" it internally because, viewed purely rationally, it can't be and, to be honest, it also isn't happening at the moment. Even after a few years, still not.
You also find yourself repeatedly involved in unpleasant and dark social issues and this won't let you live a dream life or work in a dream job. Instead, you repeatedly experience loneliness, exclusion, poverty, etc. and by doing so, you do incredibly great things with it as part of your current assignment in Project Earth.

So, it will also help you in this area if you "break apart" the individual "traces of life" and keep them apart. First of all, for your own understanding. Then also as a role model for other people, as most people have their own "own image" (neutrally speaking) of a highly developed, fully conscious person and their human life.

If you read the two aspects just described carefully, you will probably realize how incredibly challenging your life currently is. Yet, to be honest, it always has been.
And we encourage you not only to be aware of this, but also to be very conscious of the many breaks and times of withdrawal.

You need space and time with yourself in order to be able to fundamentally and well carry what you experience in many ways. And you need time to adapt well and fundamentally to all the new things.
You no longer have to work hard to get to the level you are at now. Instead, you can consciously and adequately give space, consciously experience and grasp, integrate and adapt. A slightly different focus than you were used to, so.

In your core being you are a high personality at the personal level of development of a master (or beyond) and at the same time, in this one incarnation you are "a completely normal person", usually a rather inconspicuous and withdrawn person for other people. You are both. At the same time. And in order to be fully comfortable in this big challenge, you need a very conscious transition period of inner processing and holistic adaptation.

Not only do you have to be able to deal with the challenge described in a beneficial way, you also have to have studied it in such detail that you understand it comprehensively. Also, and especially, the extremely high level of personal achievement involved in the situation in question.

You know.
You know and grasp to a degree that the average person not only cannot imagine, but the ability is far beyond what the average person can achieve in their current life.
Well, you know anyway. And this also requires a certain amount of adaptation, as the ability described is not that easy to carry.

- You know the cornerstones of your next years. Long before they arrive.
- You understand the whole person and know about their life when you meet a human counterpart. You understand his current challenges and you know about suitable solution options.
- You know what the other person is thinking, and you understand their intentions and basic attitude.
- You capture the history and challenges of teams, companies, families and entire regions. In addition, you recognize the corresponding solution options.

Knowing is a big responsibility. One that requires a corresponding level of integrity and so, you inevitably lose this ability as soon as you cannot deal with it purely and with integrity. Knowledge, actually knowledge, is only done by those people who don't talk about it.

Your human life is subject to the energy-based circumstances and the energy-based laws as soon as your holistic being is connected to the energy-based level.
During a certain transition period, however, you try to live the life you had before. Something that is no longer possible, purely objectively speaking. The material-based circumstances and laws that you were previously familiar with no longer apply. You can no longer live your life the way you used to. You first have to recognize this in order to then deal very consciously with the new way and to understand in practice what exactly is changing and how.

The aspects of your human life can no longer be classified in a human way, and they can no longer be changed in a human way. It is always the one that best serves you here and now. Regardless of whatever your human mind thinks.

You have in abundance that which meets your authentic here and now needs. Neither more nor less. Everything else continually evolves according to your respective authentic needs. And this one fact alone sometimes has to be practically "spelled out" for months until it is understood in depth. Apparently, nothing changes on the outside. At the same time, somehow everything is changing.
Yet, understanding this and then being able to live with it well over time requires a lot of personal effort and a lot of time.

If then, your consciousness expands further, you move out of the topic of energies and move into the seventh dimension and its topic of frequencies. And now, circumstances and laws are changing again. If your holistic being is then connected to the seventh dimension, you change using frequencies and no longer necessarily using thoughts / feelings (forms of energy, in the material-based human living space) or active actions. Even if you still do the latter two. Quite successful.

However, if your holistic system is subordinate to the seventh dimension, the focus and strength is now on change work using frequencies. And if you are not yet confident in the mode described, ask your own inner essential self for a comprehensive introduction so that you understand and become confident in the new. As a team member of Project Earth, you must have a comprehensive understanding of frequencies. Especially in the human context. And so, your practical life revolves around this topic for a certain period of time. Until you have mastered it sustainably.

People "commit themselves" and fight and nevertheless, often only achieve what they actually want to achieve in relative terms. We change using frequencies and do this very successfully and sustainably. We do this effortlessly and in great harmony. For the benefit of all living beings on planet Earth. And this represents a significant paradigm shift.

3.3 Frequencies

If you read the word "frequencies" from a human material-based perspective, you fill the word with an appropriate meaning. If you read the word again, this time from a vibration-based perspective, it means something completely different. Thus, in order to understand this chapter, you need a very high level of personal development in your core being, your consciousness must be completely open, and you must have mastered the vibration-based seventh dimension.
Not everyone understands the meaning that we mean when we write frequencies. We are very aware of this. And it helps you if you yourself are aware of it as well.

The situation described applies in many ways, including in the human environment. People often act as if all people were similar and that all people understand the same thing, can do the same thing and need the same thing. However, that is by no means the case. People understand according to their personal level of development. They need according to their individual needs and abilities. And they experience according to their personal navigation.

Every person is at a very individual point and brings their overall personality and corresponding abilities with them when they are born. And so, self-empowerment and individuality will be in demand in the human environment in the coming decades.

In order to understand the form of frequencies we are referring to here, you need an appropriate energy-based perception ability. If this is the case, you (also) perceive frequencies using your expanded energy-based perception abilities. Wherever you are; if you want, you can easily grasp the diverse frequencies that are there. You capture energy. You capture forms of energy. You capture energy fields. You capture vibration. And you capture frequencies.
The more your own consciousness opens, the more diverse you perceive and the more important it is that you learn to deal with the diverse and complex perceptions.
One way to do this is to concentrate on your particular focus. For example, if you completely immerse yourself in the human material-based living space and focus on your material-based senses, this almost makes you forget about your additional abilities. They are too, but you don't consciously perceive them. The situation is very similar with the area of vibration and frequencies. Once you reach a certain level of development, you notice them, but you can easily ignore them by focusing on other things.

When you move around in the human environment, a lot of things happen automatically, without you have to consciously thinking about it. This significantly simplifies human life. At the same time, it also keeps you stuck on the human material level to some extent, which isn't a bad thing in and of itself. However, as soon as you have a certain high level of personal development and an open consciousness, your awareness in this regard is required, as now, your power lies more and more on the vibration-based level. To do this, however, you have to move your focus and your perception very consciously on this level. Something that usually doesn't happen automatically but requires your conscious decision.

Frequencies are everywhere. But in the first period in which you can perceive and consciously use them, you are usually still too human and so, you usually do not perceive them to the extent to which you could (and should) perceive them now.
You know vibration and frequencies from your past lives in the vibration-based seventh dimension. At the same time, you have to get to know them a little bit new in this one human incarnation. In order to then consciously study them in the context of the human living environment.

**Frequencies are everywhere.
Yet, you have to consciously pay attention to
them, in order to be able to perceive them
consciously.**

You can only study the topic of frequencies in
the setting of the human living space by
consciously concentrating on them, observing,
recognizing and letting yourself be consciously
taught and guided by your own inner essential
self. You have to consciously deal with it, so that
you understand comprehensively and can
consciously use vibration and frequencies.

In the vibration-based dimension you control
using frequencies. At the same time, as a person,
you are used to adapting to your surroundings.
And so, it happens automatically at the
beginning that you adapt your own frequency to
your respective environment. However, from a
vibration-based perspective, this means you lose
the opportunity to have some kind of influence
and possibly even have a positive impact. On the
contrary, your surroundings have a significant
influence on you.

If you are subject to the vibration-based dimension, it is extremely unfortunate if you adapt holistically to your respective outside. Because you thereby adapt your own high vibration frequency to the respective setting. Yet, by doing so, you lose your vibration-based change ability. Moreover, you enable the respective setting to let take influence you and your life through its frequencies.

At the beginning this only happens unconsciously and so, it supports you if you consciously learn to differentiate between the levels within yourself. Begin to consciously observe yourself, guided by your own inner essential self.

Once you have reached your essential basic vibration frequency, consciously keep it stable wherever you move and focus exclusively on this one task until you have mastered it sustainably. Stay conscious of yourself and keep some holistic distance from your surroundings. Let your own inner essential self show you how energies and vibration begin to move according to your high frequency. Observe on an energy-based level and observe on a material-based level.

People focus on words, actions and measurable results. And since you are still human, your focus is naturally still on these parameters, even if you are already subordinate to the energy-based dimension.

This means that you do not perceive the power of the energy-based level or perceive it too little and therefore use it far too little. For yourself, but also for your commitment to Project Earth. And if you like, consciously allow a comprehensive introduction to this. So that you can comprehensively understand it and therefore use it comprehensively.

If you are subject to the vibration-based dimension, you know this internally pure and clearly. If so, frequencies and vibrations play a very important role in your practical life.

In a first step you will be taught to keep your own essential vibration frequency stable.
This is primarily so, that your human life can transform into an essential human life.
- Your food is designed according to your personal vibration frequency.
  This happens regardless of human nutritional recommendations. It is only the respective frequency that counts.
- If your body then transforms into a light-based human body and you are therefore subject to the ninth dimension, it is the "light portion" that defines your food intake.

- It's the same with your clothes and your home furnishings. It is vibration / frequency and over time possibly also light that defines.

If you are aware of this, you can more consciously engage with what feels right here and now.

It's your inner navigation,
that guides you correctly at all times.

At the same time, it is helpful if you fully understand why happens what happens and what attracts you. When your holistic being begins to join a higher dimension, human reasoning becomes useless. Yet, it seems important to us to emphasize again at this point: every person is different. Every person is in his or her own place. Therefore, every person needs something different. What you are reading here cannot automatically be transferred to other people. On the contrary: most people today do not understand what is written here and honestly do not need it in the course of this one human life.

The laws of the respective dimension to which the respective person is connected always apply. Most people are and remain tied and subordinated to the material-based dimension. And it stays that way throughout her life. This makes it pointless for them to deal with other dimensions. It does not serve them. Rather, it distracts them from their own material-based tasks. Others, on the other hand, are here with a specific mission and have to sustainably master not only the material-based dimension, but also the energy-based fifth dimension and the vibration-based seventh dimension.

Each of these dimensions is a whole separate dimension with its own circumstances and its own laws. It is important to be fully present again and to consciously master it in the context of human life. At the beginning, it will help you if you consciously keep the individual dimensions apart. Once you have fully recognized them, you will experience how they begin to merge into one another and how you still carry the theory behind them within you and can consciously use them at any time. You have then reached a very high holistic level, purely objectively, viewed from the outside.

People scale, evaluate and differentiate according to human material-based criteria. If you are subject to the vibration-based dimension, it will help you if you consciously stop doing it. You now attract into your life according to your essential vibrational frequency.

And even if, from a purely human perspective, your counterpart is your student or subordinate, you may be connected on an energy-based level in appreciative and supportive contact and are both aware that you both have the same essential size. This connects you in an intimacy that may never have connected you with your human family.

If you now, are aware of all levels, you can deal with it easily. However, if you try to maintain the human material-based setting in a controlling manner, you will miss out on what was actually intended to enrich both of you. Therefore, it always requires your conscious mindfulness, your conscious attention and your conscious inner dialogue. You continually find yourself in new situations as soon as your holistic being begins to connect to the energy-based dimensions. Situations in which you ideally allow yourself to be consciously guided by your own inner essential self and also allow yourself to fully recognize and understand. More and more.

Over time you realize that you can consciously change frequencies.

This is a beautiful, effortless and incredibly effective work. And it is very worthwhile to deal with it comprehensively. Until you know and master all aspects. If you like, let yourself be consciously introduced and taught by your own inner essential self.

If you are able to consciously change frequencies, increasing the frequency of your respective environment can be much more pleasant. The control of this process falls to the guidance of your own inner essential self and when you begin to consciously observe, you can easily recognize this. If you continue to observe, you will also be able to see how the respective people become essential, free and alive. Truth begins to emerge, and this enables essential and sustainable solutions.

Fictions and overlays dissolve layer by layer and this visibly relieves pressure on the individual people, but of course also on the respective setting. Your example and your attitude attract and motivate behavior changes. Wherever you move, your stay will visibly leave its mark. However, this can only be recognized based on energy and so, it supports you if you always recognize yourself comprehensively.

If you are at the personal development level of a master in your core being and your being is then subordinated to the energy-based dimension, you have the opportunity to connect with another person via your energetic heart space and thus stabilize them. A very effective type of stabilization. At the same time, you connect personally and so, the connection always costs you holistic strength. If you are then subject to the vibration-based, seventh dimension, you have the opportunity to stabilize using frequency adjustments. This form is just as effective and at the same time, you don't connect personally and so, it doesn't cost you any holistic power. You now, have the opportunity to act more effortlessly and therefore, have a more varied and comprehensive influence because your work requires less energy.

If you know within yourself that you are subject to the vibration-based seventh dimension, it is worth consciously allowing yourself to comprehensively grasp frequencies. You now have access to many additional and effortless ways to manifest and work. This significantly relieves your human self and visibly enriches your human life.

If you have also planned for a light-based human body in this one human life, it will help you if you master the seventh dimension as quickly as possible so that your holistic being can be connected to the ninth dimension and the transformation of your human body can begin. Said transformation can only begin when you are safely subordinate to the ninth dimension.

As soon as you focus your attention on your outside, your essential vibration frequency changes. If you then even relate to yourself, things change a bit. Both behaviors are typically human and so, both must (may) dissolve when you begin to live, and act based on vibrations. This in turn increases your holistic integrity and holistic immunity.

4. Leadership

As already described several times in our previous books, the human form of leadership differs significantly from the energy-based form. And it will help you if you deal with it in detail so that you can ultimately understand it comprehensively. On an energy-based level, the key to any leadership task lies in the free essential size of a personality. More precisely, in the respective frequency. In practice, this means that the free essential size and thus its stable vibration frequency must first be achieved sustainably before you can conduct energy based. Of course, you will also be in charge beforehand. Human material based with a slight blend with the energy-based form. However, you can only do this purely based on energy once you have reached your essential vibration frequency in a stable manner.

The situation described has so far been one of the main reasons why human incarnated personalities have not been in charge of energy-based projects. They could not reach their (high) essential vibrational frequency in their human embodiment. The low fundamental frequency of the earth has prevented this from happening in the long term, until now.

This has now changed drastically in the last few years. And so, not only Susanne but also several other currently humanly embodied personalities can now be found in energy-based governing bodies.

Since the number of energy-based projects on the planet as part of the overall Project Earth will increase significantly over the next few decades and the number of human embodiments in the respective governing bodies is also expected to increase significantly, we use this book to focus on the most important ones to point out differences between human forms of leadership and energy-based forms of leadership.

4.1 Selection process

Human selection processes are usually complex, diverse and lengthy.

- You need the necessary training, skills and experience.
- You must actively apply for a specific position (with a well-written CV, good references and an interesting letter of motivation).
- People in certain positions pre-select.
- You have to prove yourself in an interview or a trial work session.
- Ideally, you have the right references.

- You reflect on your own profit and your own effort and decide according to personal criteria.
- Your respective counterparts do the same.
- And once both have decided, a collaboration will happen or not.
- Of course, you can also spontaneously get together with other people and consciously set up a project group. Then the selection decides something different, but is ultimately also based on data, facts, plans, analyzes and generally valid material-based circumstances.

Energy-based happens differently. What you here need first and foremost is your free essential size so that you can even be considered for an energy-based project. Only then are you capable from an energy-based perspective. At the same time, this personal fundamental vibration frequency must be extremely high, and your integrity and holistic stability must be high and stable at all times. You must also have the diverse skills needed in the respective project. The corresponding reference is saved in your personal energy space. All your experiences and previous achievements in all your lives are stored there and can then be read in in the event of an energy-based selection.

If you qualify from an energy-based perspective, your essential self will receive an initial impulse to participate in an energy-based project. The first official request, therefore.

Your essential self now goes through an inner grid within milliseconds:
- Are you completely ready to participate in this one project?
- Does it serve you?
- Is it your job?

From an energy-based perspective, your holistic preparedness is the second most important key to participating in an energy-based project.
- You have to be well overall, and you have to be completely comfortable.
- You are not allowed to "have any construction sites" in your (human) life at the moment.
- You must be in your full strength and life energy, have abundance in every single area of your life and therefore have sufficient holistic resources.

Your leadership (or even your membership) will not take place if the points listed are not fully met.

Another important point is the fact that the mission serves you personally. Not only do you have to have sufficient holistic resources at your disposal, you also have to be able to consciously use your diverse skills and you have to benefit personally in some way.

- You can further develop your skills.
- You can have important experiences for yourself.
- You can develop holistically.
- Your holistic abundance increases through your commitment.

And because we wrote about it:

Any participation in an energy-based project guarantees you a balance that is optimally tailored to you and your current situation.

Well, participating in said project must also be your job. And this too, is consciously examined by your own inner essential self.
If it is then a holistic "yes", you can record this: You know that you have been asked for an energy-based project.
Depending on your level of personal development, you now roughly perceive this and as a rule you know to a minimum what it is about.

Now the energy-based selection process begins within the entire project team. This means that it begins to sort itself out involuntarily and without outside influence:

- The specific tasks are based on the respective competencies of the individual members.
- The hierarchy is naturally designed according to the free essential size of the members.

After a certain amount of time, you will know internally and clearly: your own position, your own task(s) and the information you need for your work.

The energy-based form of selection bypasses your human mind and will. You can neither analyze nor force. You don't have to present yourself and you don't have to reflect. It happens much more comprehensively and appropriately. If you are involved, this is done for your own highest and best and what you do within the framework of the respective project is also done for the highest and best of everything that is. On an energy-based level, questioning and human decision-making are eliminated.
What happens is right and serves as much as possible. As long as your essential size is free, and you are completely authentic.

4.2 Management function

If you are in charge of an energy-based project, you know this internally, pure and clear. Most of your team members will never know this. It doesn't matter to them who leads. The typically human form of "leadership" is missing on an energy-based level. Here every personality is fully responsible and fully in charge. External guidance, as is common among humans, do not know the energy-based dimensions.

However, you yourself know and you guide (the project) significantly via your high and pure vibrational frequency. If a person has the management function of an energy-based project, he or she has a very high level of personal development, a completely open consciousness and a very, very high level of holistic integrity. The higher the personal vibration frequency of the person leading an energy-based project, the more successful the respective project can develop. Simply because of the fact that many other project members with a very high personal vibration frequency can also contribute.

The manager of an energy-based project is therefore a central key to the success of such a project. It is primarily their free and high vibration frequency that counts.

If you are in the management role of an energy-based project, you control via vibration.
In a first step, you keep your free, essential vibration frequency stable, thereby enabling a natural order within the team and the development of a sensible structure for the project. This all happens solely because of your stable vibration frequency. Effortless and beautiful.

Contrary to many human opinions, order and the creation of helpful and healthy structures are the foundation of every successful project, even in the energy-based dimension. On the energy-based level, however, this happens independently and in accordance with the energy-based laws. All it requires is a leadership personality with a very high and pure, stable fundamental frequency. If this is present, it forms in a correspondingly healing and stable manner.

If thus, you have the management function, you consciously keep your own vibration frequency stable and consciously wait until you know internally that the hierarchy, order and structures of the project are stable.

You feel the same way as the other members of the project: you don't know most of the team members personally and you never get to know them. Nevertheless, it is your respective frequency (including your personal energy signature, of course) that guides it. Because: Every team member knows your energy signature, knows that you are leading the project (even if they do not know you personally and have not received an official personal announcement) and recognize your leadership role. A purely energy-based story that you will probably have to consciously experience a few times in order to observe what is so clearly different and then understand it over time. Ideally, this will happen in your role as a team member with significantly less responsibility. Energy-based projects are different than human projects. Therefore, you have to consciously deal with it at the beginning in order to understand it comprehensively over time.

A basic requirement for a possible management role at a later date: You must have a comprehensive understanding of the topic of energy-based projects in order to be able to take on the management role.

Well, you also have to fully understand the topic of "stable frequency" and so, we would like to make a brief digression at this point.

Excursus "stable vibration frequency"
If you are not yet sufficiently aware of the topic, your basic vibration frequency is constantly changing. These may be small changes that you may not even recognize yourself, but these fluctuations have strong effects as soon as you are subject to the vibration-based dimension. And if you like, consciously allow your own essential self to fully introduce you to the topic. You learn best in practice and to do this you have to focus your perception on certain parameters and topics. We would like to address some of them here.

Your vibration frequency adapts to your focus unless you are aware of it.
If you direct your perception towards certain topics, your vibration frequency adapts in the respective direction. This happens automatically. Until you consciously recognize the situation and consciously take countermeasures. You will find your own way of dealing with it.

I, Susanne, am trying to describe a possible variant of the procedure in human words: *Consciously keep your fundamental frequency stable and stay with part of your attention in this frequency. Now focus the rest of your attention on a topic, a task or even a person.*

You will find that you can easily keep the frequency stable in this way. Even if you simultaneously transform deep-vibrating forms of energy and immerse yourself in them with a large part of your holistic perception. This one part is important, it consciously keeps your fundamental frequency stable. Let yourself be guided by your own inner essential self, but you will see that you will succeed effortlessly.
If you now consciously observe, you will be able to see that the power of your work increases greatly through this form. You now consciously use your own high vibration frequency, and this has great power.

People with a very high level of personal development are highly capable. In an unconscious state, this often leads to them being exploited or abusing themselves. They can do it in a variety of ways, and they can do it at a high level. This usually doesn't remain hidden. At the same time, however, they often do not get back the same amount as they invest. And if the topic resonates within you, allow yourself to be resolved and clarified in the long term, so that you can be free in the long term.

If you are connected to the energy-based dimension, the area described changes greatly. You will now have more and more opportunities to use your real abilities for the benefit of humanity and the entire planet. This fulfills you holistically. At the same time, you get back according to your high stake. Outside human imagination and especially beyond human influence. And we encourage you to consciously allow yourself to consciously observe and thereby recognize more and more. This is your personal balance, and it is very high depending on your personal size and your personal commitment. Naturally.

Your main task now is to keep your own high vibration frequency stable and pure. And this will challenge you quite a bit for a while. The more aware you are that you now, have to concentrate on your own inner stability, the quicker you will find your way into the new task. The challenge is that normal human life continues as normal, and this naturally distracts you from the main task described. Especially since this doesn't officially exist in your current public human life.

The difficulty that we are currently repeatedly discussing in the management board of Project Earth is the fact that there are now more and more people who are fully aware of themselves again, are connected to the energy-based, the vibration-based or sometimes even the ninth dimension and at the same time, this is not officially known in the human habitat.
As a result, you live a kind of "shadow life": on the outside you are a completely normal person with all sorts of human tasks and at the same time you live a life that is much larger than what your fellow human beings can understand. As a result, those around you have a very limited view of who you are and what you do.

And even if the essential self of the respective people definitely understands you and shows you appreciation and the energy-based living personalities also honor you for your being and work, you still mostly do it in secret. A challenge that we are currently unable to solve satisfactorily.

The more energy-based tasks you take on and the higher and more complex they are, the more times of personal withdrawal you need to be able to carry them out. In theory, you will then be doing extremely valuable work. However, this work is currently neither financially rewarded nor otherwise waged in the human environment.
At the same time, energy-based evolution also plays a role here and so, the appreciation and honor on an energy-based level is also reflected over time in the material-based third dimension. However, not officially connected to your high and important energy-based work.

Currently only other highly developed and fully conscious people are able to establish this connection. Therefore, it currently seems as if you will have to endure the tension described for a while until we find satisfactory solutions. What we ask of you: Please recognize what great things you are doing and respect and honor your valuable actions.

From a purely human perspective, your current life seems relatively successful and rather narrow and withdrawn. At the same time, from an energy-based perspective, it is extremely powerful and successful and so, far beyond the comprehension of the average person.
Therefore, it seems important to us that at least you yourself are very conscious of what actually is.

People who manage energy-based projects are generally not involved in human management functions. Even if these people would be extremely valuable in these functions. But the management function in an energy-based project requires a lot of personal, holistic resources and a high level of holistic flexibility. This cannot currently be reconciled with human management functions. Even if you were more than capable of it. And here we close the circle opened a few pages ago: We are very aware that the energy-based management function in the human living space currently does not receive anywhere near the recognition that high human management functions receive and so, we in the management council of the Project Earth have decided that all people who hold management positions in energy-based projects should be very consciously and generously relieved and compensated.

Something you will notice clearly in the next few months. As you read these lines, please consciously refrain from getting caught up in human fantasies and instead allow yourself consciously, without any expectations. You will consciously experience and then know. It doesn't need anything more.

At the same time, we would like to point out to you that the management function of energy-based projects requires a lot of time, space and holistic personal resources. Something that you will experience clearly at the latest during your first use in this regard. And it helps you, if you are very aware of it and can then classify it accordingly in practice.

You don't have to plan, organize or control. All it requires, is your conscious surrender to your own inner essential self which will guide you perfectly and organize your human life perfectly.

The management function is the most important and by far the most complex task within an energy-based project. As a rule, you can be an active member of several energy-based projects, but not hold several related management positions. After all, you are still human and therefore still involved in a variety of human tasks. At the same time, you will be able to perceive that the focus of your (human) life is very much on your energy-based leadership function and that everything else is formed around this very valuable task.

Your human self is provided for in abundance and your human life functions externally. Nevertheless, the focus is on your essential task and this needs to be understood comprehensively as a first step.

Your human self is not asked, and it organizes itself to a certain extent "silently". This is not that easy to bear, even if you don't lose or suffer any kind of deficiency, from a purely objective point of view. It is, nonetheless. And that cannot be "glossed over".

5. Frequency increases

In the first part of this book, we dealt with the indirect forms of frequency increase. You need this knowledge as a basis for the forms of direct frequency increase. Please be aware that this requires conscious and clear permission from the Council of Light and a personal connection to the ninth dimension. Something you know inside, pure and clear, if so. If you do not have this knowledge within you, you may skip this chapter because it is not written for you and thus will not serve you.

If you carry the knowledge described within you, you will reach a point where you realize that you can consciously change frequencies. Not just your own, but also other people's frequencies, especially those in your immediate surroundings.
You enter the respective frequency with your conscious attention and are able to consciously change it. Usually you increase it a little, then consciously wait a few days, observe and allow yourself to be guided internally. Once you have reached the point described, you can change effortlessly and highly effectively. However, for this you need an extremely high level of integrity, as your actions have a strong impact on the respective environment and the planetary balance.

Therefore, you don't just increase and then move on, but you stay very consciously in the area or topic in which you increased the frequency, observe comprehensively and continually adjust the frequency. We don't want to cause any unrest or any harm with this action and so, it requires a very conscious and careful approach.

You probably guessed it: this work also requires a lot of holistic resources, and this work is neither recognized nor rewarded by human society. This is despite the fact that there are currently only a few people who are capable of it and the global impact is enormously beneficial. Yet, and in return you are repeatedly removed from human obligations, but also from human pleasures. Guided into personal retreat and holistically shielded for your important work. And when you recognize the truth of your so important actions, you will, on the one hand, work further full of gratitude. On the other hand, you also look now and then at your fellow human beings wistfully and perhaps a little envious from time to time. When they celebrate parties, go on vacation, ride their bikes, etc.

Of course, you will also experience things that you like and that enrich you. But to be honest, they only happen in small doses. So that you are enriched and can (briefly) enjoy. After that, however, you will very quickly be involved in your essential tasks again, as they are very important, at the moment. And so, we can't afford to take very long breaks, now.
And what we write here is truth. Unadorned. Not very human. Because you carry a lot, and you are only allowed to enjoy the beauties and comforts of human life "bit by bit". Therefore, at least where possible, you should receive as much positivity as possible.

The conscious increase in frequency often follows similar patterns.

- You consciously increase and can observe how everything living in the respective environment breathes a sigh of relief and is comfortable.
- Then you very consciously lower yourself a little bit again because the negative energy forms and energy fields in the respective personal energy spaces, but also in the energy space of the respective region, begin to loosen and show themselves.

- If you are able to reduce in a very targeted manner, it will only become moderately restless in the region and the first negative energy fields and forms of energy can be acted out and dissolved independently.
- Now you increase something again, observe, stabilize and very consciously transform everything dark and negative that you encounter.
- Then you lower yourself again and thereby stabilize and calm down in a very targeted manner.

Now there is an initial break of several weeks to observe and stabilize. But also, to keep a very conscious eye on the regional effects. You don't do this alone, but in collaboration with a variety of energy-based living personalities who are specially trained for this task. This means you continually receive information that is important to you, collect it and, if necessary, react in a stabilizing and calming manner.

Well, over time you will also "heal" people and by doing so, very consciously accompany them back to holistic health. In said work, you use the same process / procedure that we just described. You increase the frequency of the system, then lower it again. You transform the darkness and negativity that the human being himself is unable to transform, you increase again, stabilize, etc. Until the holistic system can completely regenerate itself.

You may only need to do the process consciously a few times, but over time you will recognize and do it effortlessly. People are only in their full power when their holistic system is healed. Some currently very highly developed people need external support during a certain phase in order to reach the described state. And so, you (and everyone who holds the same task) will very consciously support these people. So, that they can reach their essential strength and thereby be able to carry out their essential tasks.

You probably guessed it: your work in this regard is also one of those things that is currently not (yet) recognized or even appreciated by human society. And therefore, for the next few years you will lead a life that continually brings you into contact with those people and those regions that need your vibration-based support.

You do this unnoticed by those around you, embedded in human settings and topics that serve your essential work. The focus is always on your essential tasks, and, from a purely human perspective, you do not always receive the compensation that you would actually be entitled to. However, if you expand your perception, you will find that you still experience a maximum of fullness and balance. The one that enriches and fulfills you here and now.
It will help you if you are aware of the situation described. So that you yourself recognize and know how extremely valuable your work is. Even and especially when those around you don't understand.

5.1 Frequency increase in the context of light technology

Light likes virtuosity and light combines wonderfully with the frequencies in masterful play. If you are not or do not behave in a masterful manner, light eludes you. These parameters are the basis for possible effects with light in the context of frequency increases. Light technology means the conscious creation of something healing with the help of light. Frequency increases basically serve the good and healing. Therefore, the two forms fit together wonderfully, as long as they are performed masterfully. Something that you must have acquired over the course of many other lives in order to be able to use it in this one human life. You can tell whether you are at the (high) skill level described by the fact that light approaches you when you consciously increase frequencies. You then, can not only perceive light, you also realize that the frequencies involuntarily feel different. They become purer and clearer, connecting with light.

Yet, the connection described carries with it the challenge of destabilizing you holistically. And so, your first task is to ensure stability: within yourself, in your respective environment and ultimately, in the connection itself.

The (high) art is, first of all, to ensure stability. Triple stability. This not only requires a high level of personal development and awareness, but also the ability to have a strong and calm presence in your own high fundamental vibration frequency. You will realize how demanding this task is in direct experience and you will probably have to consciously experience it a few times, so that you can see what we mean by the words we have just written.

Light recognizes your true nature. Yet, it recognizes your level of development and your abilities. Light works with you when you have a very high level of personal development and purity and very high abilities. You don't need any external reputation for this. Light captures and knows. And if you work together with light, you not only need your essential vibration frequency to be stable and freely present, you also need your true being to be stable and freely present. A being that is extremely sovereign and capable. Far beyond anything a human mind is capable of imagining.

If you are one of the (few) people who actively work with light and are capable of the highest possible level of light technology, it is imperative that your true being is stable and free. Even if you move in a completely normal human way, integrated into a completely normal human setting.

You have to first recognize this and then, consciously allow it. And if you like, ask your own inner essential self to teach you and implement the state described.

Light needs a counterpart.
A free, sovereign and capable counterpart.

This is who you are when your true being is freely and stably present. You will realize that this state is once again far above your fundamental frequency state. And during a certain adaptation phase, the state described will "visit" you in phases, which you can tell by the fact that this severely destabilizes you holistically.

You then, need all of your stabilization skills to remain somewhat stable and you will only be so, when your being dims down a bit again. This will happen to you repeatedly over a few weeks. Whenever you are not absolutely needed. Over time, you will notice that you destabilize less and are able to bear the situation increasingly better. This is an extremely intensive and challenging process that should be appreciated. Much more however, to be grasped and understood.

Otherwise, you will become very insecure because you cannot understand what is repeatedly destabilizing you without being able to cope with it. However, once you have recognized it, it is important to consciously stabilize and persevere a bit, because your holistic system is able to adapt independently over time and you are therefore able to grow stably into the new state.

After that you are: your true essence. Free and stable. And then, you have to learn to recognize what this means in practical terms for your current life.

Active work in the field of light technology in the human habitat is only possible as a human, if you have a completely converted human light body. However, this is only possible if your entire being is connected to the ninth dimension of planet Earth. Which in turn means that your true being is free and stable in its entirety. A condition that can hardly be put into words and takes time to adapt to well and stably.

You will probably find that it is much easier for you to achieve the described state and keep it stable in your own four walls. If you then go into human society, you must consciously learn to keep it stable there too. You will be able to observe that this irritates your personal environment, as you are and behave visibly differently than before.

You can now neither dim nor hide your true nature. It is. Clearly noticeable. Pure and clear. What most people are convinced that such a thing is not possible: A thoroughly pure person with integrity. A person who can no longer be dominated or manipulated. A person who is always safe to be with, but who also challenges with his purity and clarity.

6. Some final words

If your holistic connection to the energy-based level changes, the laws and circumstances to which you are subject change. This reads logically and can then be experienced practically in a comprehensible manner over time.
However, it can happen that you repeatedly "stumble" over certain topics that slow you down overall. And we would like to consciously address this in this chapter.

Your previous human thinking and your previous experiences shape you, your current thinking, your current experience, your current actions and especially your current expectations.
Especially because you move around the human environment in a continuous association.

- You think, plan and act according to a linear understanding of time. You repeatedly think forward and draw conclusions for your future based on your current here and now, based on human assessments and your previous experiences.
This behavior is harming you!! Please leave it now at the latest. You are completely subject to the energy-based circumstances and the energy-based laws.

- If you have a lot, you have to give a lot. If you are very resilient, you have to carry a lot. Mostly without you getting anything in return. These typically human experiences leave clear traces. Therefore, it is important to work through them consciously.
So that you can freely and calmly engage with your essential size and all its implications. As already written: You are now subject to the energy-based laws and whoever carries a lot receives a lot. Naturally.

- During a certain phase, you are usually far too unaware of how important it is to give truth space within yourself very consciously and completely. You know the truth, but as long as you don't consciously allow it to take up full space within yourself, it cannot develop its true power. If you are unsure about a certain situation, consciously speak "truth and clarity" about it and consciously work on it within yourself until you know it. Then consciously give it space within yourself and allow it to adapt accordingly.
You usually don't have to do anything active. Just consciously allow yourself to take up space.

- It can only develop what you carry pure and clearly within you. Here and now. To do this, you must have consciously worked on all levels of a topic so that they all appear congruent. Only then can it manifest accordingly. This topic also needs to be studied and understood comprehensively.
- You often capture an aspect of your front and then intuitively relate it to a typical human setting. You realize that you will have your own house, for example. And now you're calculating wildly in your head whether something like this is financially possible. A very, very small one, at most? No matter how hard you calculate, it doesn't add up in your human thinking. And what we describe here as an example can be transferred to all possible aspects: You have a short, clear impulse within yourself and then try to implement it using your human thinking. Something that no longer works. Because development is now based on energy. Much more appropriate, much more comprehensive and much different than you could humanly imagine or even organize.

And this is where the next point fits very well.

If you are no longer comfortable with the here and now, you need to deal with it in a significantly different way than you were previously used to.
If a person is no longer comfortable with the here and now, they usually go intuitively into their imagination and look for what could feel good instead. And what "feels good" there, in your head, usually doesn't really have much connection to your here and now. Well, a person doesn't know any different and once he has found a mentally appealing image, he then usually becomes active outside and tries to change his now in the direction of his image. Sometimes he succeeds, sometimes not. You yourself are also human and so, the behavior described is not only very familiar to you, rather it is still with you and within you. Therefore, we would like to encourage you not only to be aware of this, but also to actively deal with it. To consciously leave your old behavior behind you and engage in behavior that corresponds to the energy-based circumstances and laws.

What could something like that look like?
First, go very consciously into your current here and now and allow yourself to fully recognize why you are not feeling well. Consciously allow yourself to grasp all levels and give yourself enough time to do so. Do this as often and for as long as it takes until you feel calm within yourself. You will permanently block yourself and your progress if you do not carry out this first step properly. Energy-based can only continue when things have been cleaned up on all levels. If this is the case, you know this internally, purely and clearly. You can also recognize the condition by the fact that you feel OK internally. Learn about the fact that change is allowed. Once it has been clarified sustainably, the next important step usually occurs to you involuntarily: you find yourself stable in your own essential vibration frequency and at the same time very consciously and mindfully fully immersed in the situation that can now change. Now very consciously resist the temptation to go into your head and develop mentally there. Instead, stay with your full attention in your essential vibrational frequency and in the corresponding situation.

If you consciously keep your human mind switched off, you will now encounter individual fragments: images, feelings, inner knowledge, etc. Colorfully mixed, still somewhat disordered, but at the same time extremely fitting.

Your entire being involuntarily breathes a sigh of relief in the new, even if it is just emerging within you. Please resist any urge you may have to get caught up in mental images and shape them using human imagination. Instead, allow yourself to evolve into the highest and best of all that is. Free and optimally suited to you.

On an energy-based level, the primary focus is not on the result, but primarily on a pure and clear output frequency. This frequency determines the respective result. Therefore, you have to go through an inner paradigm shift (including the corresponding conscious discussion) in order to understand things better, step by step. Pay conscious attention to your here and now and bring it into contact with your pure personal vibration frequency as often as possible. In this way, development continues naturally without you being unnecessarily blocked or having to make unnecessary holistic "curves".

The compensation for your valuable work is done holistically and optimally adapted to you. As a human being, you are used to certain material-based parameters and so, your focus in this regard is logically very much on these (few) parameters. However, what is now happening is much more comprehensive and sustainable and this too needs to be understood in depth. If you like, allow appropriate introduction from your own inner essential self. Your understanding of this will automatically expand your perspective and your recognition will strengthen your knowledge and security.

To work great, you need a strong and secure human foundation. You must be comfortable and secure in your current human life, in your current human relationships, and in your current human tasks. Your finances must be sustainably safe and healthy. And, you have to feel completely comfortable in your human body. If you recognize that this is not yet the case, ask your own inner essential self for clear guidance. Ultimately, you need a completely essential human life in order to be able to devote yourself to your essential tasks unencumbered and thereby in your full strength. Yet, you lead an essential human life when every little aspect of your current human life corresponds to your essential vibrational frequency.

This fact makes you feel completely comfortable. A feeling that you as a human being generally do not know and can honestly never achieve under the current conditions that prevail in the human environment. However, if you have sustainably achieved your essential vibration frequency in this one human life (worked on it with a lot of sweat, formulated more honestly) and if you have set yourself essential tasks for this one human incarnation, something that has never happened before will take place in the human living space.

Thanks to the decision of the Council of Light formulated in the book "Intercultural Mediation – Volume 1" and the increasing support of the energy-based kingdoms, you can also reach the described state more quickly and effortlessly. We urgently need your free and powerful work and so, your fully essential life ultimately supports the positive effect of Project Earth.

**You can only fully devote yourself to the energy-based dimension and your essential tasks,
when you are completely comfortable and secure in your current human life.**

If this is not the case yet, it will block you again and again. Therefore, we ask you to take this aspect very seriously.

In the energy-based living space, the focus is on the personality itself and its own well-being. And this also represents a clear paradigm shift, when your holistic being is connected to the energy-based dimension. At the same time, this aspect underlines the truth that you are only in your full power and strength, when you are completely comfortable. And so, we encourage you to consciously devote yourself to this topic, until you have studied and grasped it sufficiently.

Ultimately, you are only fully comfortable in your human life, if it essentially corresponds to you in every single area.

People sometimes need to consciously address their own authentic needs over an extended period of time. They have forgotten how to perceive these and sometimes even how to have their own needs.
At the same time, you must be aware that you are subordinate to the energy-based dimension, and it is your free and stable essential vibrational frequency that realizes accordingly.

A person often gives on the outside, what he should actually give himself.

And if you occasionally feel the urge to give something specific to another person, it can make sense to look very consciously and attentively, and consciously clarify whether you are still missing something in any area of your life. We are aware that we are repeating ourselves: But it is your complete, holistic fullness that must now be in the foreground so that you can work freely and with all your strength.

If you take up space in the human habitat in your entire size, you run the risk of taking space away from other people. In the energy-based dimension, however, you must very consciously take up space in your entire size so that you can organize yourself in a way that is beneficial and full for those around you. And this paradigm shift may also have to be consciously experienced in practice a few times until it can be understood in depth. Once you have understood, it will be easier for you to consciously take up space in your entire size and with all your abilities.

From an outside perspective, Project Earth has developed extremely well. The frequency was increased stably for the first time in all regions of the world and the corresponding side effects were minimized to the maximum and are under control. A different picture may appear to you in the human environment itself, we are very aware of that.

Old, dark and negative forms of energy are now continually rising, and some unpleasant things are being acted out repeatedly. At the same time, these are natural side effects of the global frequency increase, and it helps if you record them as such.

Of course, we are also aware that we are still far from where we will eventually be. At the same time, we didn't know whether we would get to the point where we are now. We are now there faster than expected and so, there is great joy on planet Earth itself, as well as in a large part of the universe. We have achieved a lot, and we are stable and doing well. Although there is of course still a lot to do.

The founding of SEOS can already be described as a very big win over the last few decades. A challenging story, as the fronts between certain living spaces and realms have been very hardened and closed in recent centuries. Some personalities have made a special contribution here and have achieved something special and we would like to thank them very much at this point.

SEOS has developed extremely positively. All realms and habitats on earth could be integrated and now, there are more and more realms that recognize and appreciate the great achievements of highly developed people and thereby, also agree to consciously support these people and their challenging work.

The energy-based realm of the dragons was there right from the start and provided extremely valuable and generous support. Surprisingly, the realm of the elves followed suit and thanks to their active and very helpful support, Project Earth has once again gained considerable strength.

Atlantis has now officially committed itself to supporting the highly developed humans themselves and their work in the human habitat and we also greatly appreciate this decision. The corresponding operation began a few weeks ago (July 24) and so, it is very possible that you will repeatedly be able to consciously perceive the energy of Atlantis around you. If it feels right for you, consciously allow: your personal support, but also support in your essential tasks. You should be relieved, and you should be supported. This basic attitude has now taken up more and more space in the energy-based realms and we are very happy about that.

It is the conscious and highly developed people who achieve extremely great things, and it is they who carry an enormous amount. Therefore, these very important key people should be given maximum support and maximum compensation. Here and now.

At the same time, each realm that is actively involved naturally also supports with its very specific gifts and priorities.

Atlantis carries the former history within itself and with it the relevant knowledge. At that time, Atlantis perfected human life at the intersection of material-based and energy-based living space. A point that we would like to reach again – among other things – in the human living space. And so, the energy of Atlantis surrounds you on the one hand to support you personally, but on the other hand also very consciously to provide you with appropriate information. We will next publish two more books in which we will structure and formulate the knowledge described in human words and thereby provide even more specific support and equipment. At the same time, you are more than capable of absorbing the corresponding energy-based information and using it in a targeted manner. Allow yourself to recognize and grasp, and it will happen to you.

At the end of this book, we would like to emphasize it again very consciously and very clearly:

Please be aware that in the next few weeks you will have to focus on yourself:

- You need abundance in every single area of your current human life.
- You need fundamental and sustainable security in every single area of your current human life.
- You must be completely comfortable in your current human life.
- You need to know your current essential tasks and become confident in carrying them out.

Please don't read too quickly over the lines just written. Instead, allow it to happen to you. An abundance that you can neither mentally imagine nor practically organize. Such stable security in every area of your current human life that you no longer have to worry about security. Yet, a great clarity: in your current human life, in your human and essential tasks and with a view to your next one.

In order to function to the extent that you are capable of, your human self must also be completely whole. And this is probably the most strenuous part of the entire story: you have to consciously work through and resolve all the many injuries. Something that has never happened before in human history: people who are completely whole / holistic healed and remain whole / holistic healed.

These people naturally have great purity, great integrity, great strength and great power. They naturally attract and they naturally become a projection surface for their fellow human beings. Challenges that need to be overcome. Even if you have a light-based human body and are subordinate to the ninth dimension. Human behavior is often perverted and hurtful in many ways and this will probably only change "incrementally" over the next few decades and that is how you will come across it again and again. Thanks to your light-based body, you are "completely immune and protected". Yet, thanks to your very high fundamental frequency, you are also very, very sensitive.
The harshness of the human environment is much easier to endure when a person has a low vibration frequency. He is then either unable to consciously perceive the harsh energies or they are so familiar to him that he perceives them as normal.

We are currently discussing a lot about what exactly people with a light-based human body and a connection to the ninth dimension need, and what they can bear. Human society would benefit immensely if said people occupied high key positions in certain areas. At the same time, they then have to make a name for themselves and are therefore publicly exposed to all kinds of human bad behavior. Something that isn't good for them.

And so, the discussions are currently moving in the direction of creating small experimental situations and consciously gathering relevant experiences there, in a not-so-public setting. These experimental situations can be broken off at any time without attracting social attention. Yet, we can keep our full attention on the respective key person, provide them with maximum support and protection and consciously remove them as soon as they should be harmed in any way.

Nevertheless, we are all very cautious and not yet really ready to put these situations into practice. The last centuries still weigh on our minds and we have no intention of repeating them even remotely. The time of human martyrs is definitely over, and it should stay that way! This makes us all very sensitive to this issue and we will do everything we can to ensure that human members of Project Earth no longer even come close to this issue.

When reading the lines just written, it may happen that something resonates within you again, as you have probably also experienced what has been described in one or more of your previous human lives. And if this is the case, we ask you to consciously and sustainably process and resolve it. So that nothing depends on you anymore.

Your holistic being repeatedly changes dimensions. Depending on your needs.
If you are not aware of this, this (new) situation is not only very confusing, but also extremely draining.
You have to know the individual dimensions very well in order to continually recognize where exactly you currently are and why you are acting from this level.
If you speak from the fifth energy-based or even seventh vibration-based dimension, a person who experiences themselves completely in the third material-based dimension cannot understand you. Maybe individual fragments will get through to him. Especially if he has a high level of personal development at his core being. However, if you want to communicate with him in a purposeful and fulfilling way, you thus, have to do so completely from the third material-based dimension. Using appropriate words.

Highly developed, fully conscious people respond intuitively from the dimension from which they are addressed. They change fluently and usually with unconscious competence. However, such people are not found very often at the moment. Therefore, it requires appropriate awareness on your part. If you begin to consciously observe, you will be able to see that you often formulate from the fifth dimension, that the person you are talking to clearly does not understand you and at the same time you realize that what is happening here and now is correct. What you said was received, even if the human mind of your counterpart clearly didn't understand it.

If you now bear the discrepancy very consciously, you will experience that the energy-based evolution supports and the words you formulated take up space and have an effect. Despite it.
Your words have triggered a positive energy shift from an energy-based perspective. One that will also show up on a materially based human level. Unfortunately, not immediately, but over time. Therefore, it helps you if you expand your own perspective a little in similar situations and consciously look at them from an energy-based perspective. Whatever you do or say has a lasting positive impact.

However, you very often act from the fifth or even seventh dimension into the third material-based human situation. It is actually logical that you are not always understood there. To be honest, you don't have to. The energy shift works independently. Positive and sustainable.

The more conscious you become,
it is all the more important that
you understand the theory
behind every single dimension.

Thus, it will help you, if you consciously know at all times that you are constantly changing dimensions, even when you are completely integrated into the materially based human living space.

If you work in the area of intercultural mediation and therefore for SEOS, the awareness described is a basic requirement for the next step: You live and work in the human habitat in a human role and at the same time act in an energy-based manner connected to individual realms and their abilities for the benefit of the Earth project. A topic that we will explore in our next book.

Until then: Take care!